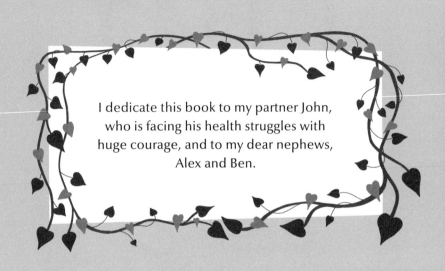

I dedicate this book to my partner John,
who is facing his health struggles with
huge courage, and to my dear nephews,
Alex and Ben.

LIST
happy

by **Vanessa KING**

Illustrated by TASHA GODDARD

Editor Caroline West
Designer Isabelle Merry
Proofreader Claire Nottage
Senior Production Editor Siu Yin Chan
Senior Production Controller Louise Minihane
Managing Editor Pete Jorgensen
Managing Art Editor Jo Connor
Publishing Director Mark Searle

First American Edition, 2022
Published in the United States by DK Publishing
1450 Broadway, Suite 801, New York, NY 10018

A catalog record for this book is available from the Library of Congress.
ISBN 978-0-7440-5789-8

DK books are available at special discounts when purchased in bulk for sales
promotions, premiums, fund-raising, or educational use. For details, contact:
DK Publishing Special Markets, 1450 Broadway, Suite 801, New York, NY 10018
SpecialSales@dk.com

Printed and bound in Slovakia.

For the curious
www.dk.com

Contents

Introduction

What makes you really happy and helps you stay that way?

Many things have an impact on how happy we feel, of course, and we can't change all of these. However, studies show[1] that what we focus on, how we think, and what we do can all make a difference—which is good news, as these are more within our control, once we know how.

In recent years, psychologists, neuroscientists, and other researchers have been studying happiness and how we can cultivate it in our own lives and for others. This book is based on that growing body of science. It's packed full of lists, tips, reflection prompts for you to explore what you think, and practical ideas for taking action, so you'll have a toolkit to help you maintain happiness and boost it when you need to.

Your happiness matters

Being happy doesn't just feel good—it also helps us to function well. Studies show that it has many potential positive benefits—for example, for our physical health, our performance in education and at work, how much we help others, and our contribution to our communities.[2] So, happiness isn't just the outcome of things going well in life, it actually contributes to this.

Unpacking happiness

There's more to being happier than we might usually think. Pleasure—that is, feeling good in the moment—is part of it and there are different types of pleasant emotions and different thoughts and actions that lead to this.

Another important aspect of being happier is having a sense of meaning and purpose in life.[3] Cultivating this doesn't always feel good at the time—you may be working hard toward a goal, learning something new, nurturing relationships, or struggling through a difficult challenge—but it can help us feel fulfilled over time.

Experiencing both pleasurable emotions and meaning are part of living a happy life. In this book, we'll explore how you can cultivate both to feel happier. Importantly, living a happier life doesn't mean we'll never feel unhappy. Everyone has ups and downs—difficulties are a part of life. The lists, reflections, and activities we'll cover together can also help you to cope when times are tough and increase your resilience, too.

What does happiness mean to you?

Brainstorm some ideas and then list them here:

_____

_____

_____

_____

_____

_____

_____

_____

Reflection

Consider what you already do to help boost and maintain your happiness?

The Power of
Feel-Good Emotions

By their very nature, emotions are fleeting, but these moments all add up. Triggered by what we perceive in the moment, emotions are more than just feelings, however. They are rapid signals from the more primitive part of our brain, based on instant, instinctive interpretations, usually about why something is happening or what might happen as a result. Different emotions have associated "action tendencies," which prepare the body for action. For example, when we feel fear, our body prepares to fight, flee, or freeze.

While the action tendencies associated with more pleasant emotions may be less immediately apparent, the psychobiologist Dr. Barbara Fredrickson and her team have shown that when we experience pleasant or positive emotions, there are also physiological responses. Our perceptual fields broaden briefly. This causes us to be more open and trusting of others and more open to new ideas. We also see more options and become better at creative problem-solving. This creates more pleasant emotional experiences and over time builds our psycho-social resources, so boosting our resilience. Regularly experiencing pleasant emotions can buffer or even help undo the harmful effects of stress. In this way, cultivating our happiness isn't only about feeling good, it's about functioning well, too.[4]

The broaden, build, and buffer effect of pleasurable feelings can help us as we work toward cultivating meaning. As noted earlier, doing things that are meaningful doesn't always feel good, so finding ways to experience moments of pleasure along the way can really help. There are lots of ideas in this book to try to help you cultivate a range of different pleasurable emotions,[5] as well as meaning.

What different feel-good emotions can you think of?

Brainstorm some ideas and then list them here:

_____

_____

_____

_____

_____

_____

_____

_____

_____

_____

_____

_____

_____

_____

Categorizing Emotions

Researchers typically categorize emotions as being either positive (feels good) or negative (feels bad), but I prefer to use the terms "pleasant" and "unpleasant." This is because unpleasant emotions like fear, anger, or sadness may not feel good, but they are not always negative. For example, it is appropriate to feel anger when we see or experience injustice or violation; to feel fear when we are in danger; or sad when we have lost someone or something dear to us.

Happiness Check-In

Take a few moments to capture how you've been feeling recently using the two sets of questions given here. You might want to come back to the questions from time to time to help you check in on how you are feeling.

1. How happy have you been feeling in general?

For each of the questions below, circle your answers on a scale of 0 to 10, where 0 is "Not At All" and 10 is "Completely." These are the four questions that the UK Government[6] regularly asks a sample of the population to measure what is known as "subjective well-being." Increasingly, other countries are introducing similar measures.

Measure	Question
Life Satisfaction	Overall, how satisfied are you with your life nowadays?
	1 2 3 4 5 6 7 8 9 10
Worthwhile	Overall, to what extent do you feel that the things you do in life are worthwhile?
	1 2 3 4 5 6 7 8 9 10
Happiness	Overall, how happy did you feel yesterday?
	1 2 3 4 5 6 7 8 9 10
Anxiety	Overall, how anxious did you feel yesterday?
	1 2 3 4 5 6 7 8 9 10

2. Types of happiness you've recently experienced

Mark the extent to which you've recently experienced each of the emotions or forms of happiness below. Circle your answers on a scale of 0 to 10, where 0 is "Not At All" and 10 is "A Lot."

Type of Happiness	To What Extent Have I Experienced This Recently?									
Gratitude	1	2	3	4	5	6	7	8	9	10
Joy	1	2	3	4	5	6	7	8	9	10
Peace	1	2	3	4	5	6	7	8	9	10
Curiosity	1	2	3	4	5	6	7	8	9	10
Pride	1	2	3	4	5	6	7	8	9	10
Amusement	1	2	3	4	5	6	7	8	9	10
Awe	1	2	3	4	5	6	7	8	9	10
Love	1	2	3	4	5	6	7	8	9	10
Hope	1	2	3	4	5	6	7	8	9	10
Meaning	1	2	3	4	5	6	7	8	9	10

Reflection

There's a chapter for each of the forms of happiness in the table above. Reflecting on your answers, what areas are you most curious to explore? List your thoughts below:

Emotions Check-In

Sometimes, reflecting back doesn't capture the full range of our emotional experiences or their fleeting, changing nature. Try this activity to explore your emotional experiences in a single day.

Pick a day and chart the emotions you feel during your waking hours. Set an hourly reminder to check in on how you are feeling and note the emotion down, along with one thing that's contributed to it.

Time	Emotion	One Thing Contributing to How I'm Feeling
9am		
10am		
11am		
12am		
1pm		
2pm		
3pm		
4pm		
5pm		
6pm		
7pm		
8pm		
9pm		

How many different emotions did you feel? What was the balance between pleasant and unpleasant emotions? The lists in this book will help you find ways to boost pleasant emotions and can help when you're not feeling happy.

How to Use This Book

This book is for you to use actively. I hope it will provide you with food for thought and ideas for action to help you live a happy life. Importantly, you'll get the most from it if, as you complete the lists and reflections, you put the ideas into practice in your life.

You don't need to work through the chapters sequentially. Or even work though them all. A suggestion is to start with some of the lists in this Introduction, then pick an emotion or type of happiness (see the *Happiness Check-In,* on page 11) you want to cultivate and explore the lists in that chapter. If you are short on time, just start by picking one list and giving it a go.

There are three different types of lists:

 Think about it lists: For you to explore your thoughts, experiences, and ideas

 Checklists: To tick off what applies to you or things that you've tried

 Action lists: To compile and do

You'll find that some lists and actions will be quick to complete, while others you may want to reflect on and add to over time. Using a notebook as a journal will allow you to expand on your thoughts and repeat or extend the lists—studies show[7] that writing things down can help us process our thoughts and in itself boosts our well-being, so a notebook will ensure you have space to do this. You'll also find lots of reflection prompts to help you as you explore your thoughts, experiences, and ideas.

Let's get started!

Gratitude

Gratitude is considered an important key to unlocking a happier life. Not only does being grateful usually feel good in the moment, but it also has many other benefits. Individually we may experience the following: more pleasant emotions, greater optimism and higher life satisfaction; lower levels of stress in response to difficulties; feeling more willing to seek help when we need it; and better sleep, physical health, and recovery from trauma.[8]

Gratitude has also been shown to boost our relationships and sense of connection to others, both vital ingredients for happiness. Studies show that gratitude increases our generosity and compassion, while also making us more likely to help others. It can also contribute to us being less materialistic and envious.[8]

Gratitude is thought to have two components: consciously noticing and acknowledging both what is good and what we value—or what has helped us—and the source(s) of these positives.[9]

Feeling gratitude helps us to feel happier. The human brain naturally focuses on what's wrong, so actively practicing gratitude, such as through the lists and activities in this chapter, can also help us notice and benefit from what's good in our lives and what is going right.[10]

Often, the sources of what we feel grateful for are outside of us—something or someone else. So, in this way, gratitude connects us to the world and those around us, helping us to feel less alone and part of something bigger. Indeed, gratitude is regarded as a social glue since it facilitates social support and connection. However, it is important to note that for gratitude to contribute to happiness, it should not create a burden of indebtedness.[11]

Our personalities vary in our natural disposition toward gratitude, but studies show that with intention and practice we can cultivate a greater capacity for it.[12] Experiment with the different ideas in this chapter and see what you notice yourself.

Who Are You Grateful To?

List five people who have made a positive difference in your life? What are you grateful to them for?

Name	How They Made a Difference to You
1	
2	
3	
4	
5	

Take Action

Write a letter to someone on your list who you've perhaps never thanked. Let them know the difference they've made to you. If you can, deliver the letter in person and read it to them.[13]

Three Good Things

This is a classic positive psychology activity. Studies have found[14] that people who did this each night for a week were happier and less likely to feel down up to six months later. Give it a go and see what you notice.

Here's how to do it. Reflect on your day yesterday: list three things you enjoyed, were pleased about, or grateful for, and (if you can) why they were good. Then repeat through the week.

Monday

1
2
3

Tuesday

1
2
3

Wednesday

1
2
3

Thursday

1
2
3

Friday

1 _____

2 _____

3 _____

Saturday

1 _____

2 _____

3 _____

Sunday

1 _____

2 _____

3 _____

Helpful Hints

- Your good things don't have to be big—in fact, they can be small or fleeting moments like noticing birds singing, the sun coming out, getting a seat on the bus, or progressing with a project. Even on tough days, try to find moments that were better than the rest.

- Try this activity just before you go to bed (keep this book or some paper and a pen on your nightstand).

- Experiment by trying the activity at different times of day and sharing good things with family or friends.

Reflection

Look back over your good things from the week. What do you notice? How did this activity feel for you?

A Week of Good Things

This weekly reflection is an alternative to the previous daily gratitude list. Experiment with both and see which one works best for you. Each week, for the next six weeks, reflect back on the last seven days, then identify five things you enjoyed, were pleased about, or grateful for, and why.[15]

Week 1

1
2
3
4
5

Week 2

1
2
3
4
5

Week 3

1
2
3
4
5

Week 4

1
2
3
4
5

Week 5

1
2
3
4
5

Week 6

1
2
3
4
5

Helpful Hint

You'll get most benefit from this activity if you try it for a few
weeks. Why not schedule a regular slot in your calendar?

100 Gratitudes

Think back over your life to date. What are 100 things you are grateful for, both large and small? List people, places, events, the world around you, your time in history... think expansively and list whatever comes to mind. Be as specific as you can.

1	21	41
2	22	42
3	23	43
4	24	44
5	25	45
6	26	46
7	27	47
8	28	48
9	29	49
10	30	50
11	31	51
12	32	52
13	33	53
14	34	54
15	35	55
16	36	56
17	37	57
18	38	58
19	39	59
20	40	60

Helpful Hints

61	81
62	82
63	83
64	84
65	85
66	86
67	87
68	88
69	89
70	90
71	91
72	92
73	93
74	94
75	95
76	96
77	97
78	98
79	99
80	100

- This can be a really thought-provoking exercise and a great one to start when you have a few moments to yourself at home or in a café.

- Don't try to think of 100 things in one go. Once you've made a start, just add to your list when things come to mind. Try to finish the list over a week or two.

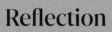

Reflection

Look back over your list and notice how you feel when you reflect on all the things you're grateful for.

Joy

What is joy? Regarded as fundamental to human existence,[16] surprisingly it's only recently that psychologists have started studying it in depth. This is perhaps because we often conflate the word "joy" with the more general term "happiness," yet it is a distinct form of positive emotional experience. Think about how you feel on receiving a nice surprise or good news out of the blue; when watching a young child delight in discovering something new; the sight of the first spring flowers after the winter; arriving in a landscape of beauty (for me, that's the azure blue seas and sky of the Aegean); or getting together with dear friends after a long time apart.

What characterizes joy is the awareness that we're experiencing something good, which we regard as a "gift" of some sort. This might be unexpected or something we've been longing for. Joy connects us to others or the world around us, and helps us in the moment to transcend our worries and concerns. When we experience joy, we momentarily feel safe, freer, or more open, and it can bring about physiological changes such as experiencing easier movement, seeing colors as being brighter, and smiling involuntarily.[17] It can even feel spiritual.[18]

Of course, like most emotions, joy can vary in magnitude, from a quiet joy to elation. There's also a moral component to it— ancient literature and religious texts warn against feeling joy at another's misfortune. Joy can provide motivation and energy for action. It can also be contagious, as we can experience joy at seeing that of others, and they at seeing ours.[19]

Finding small moments or sources of joy can also help us in tougher times. A good friend of mine, artist Linda Bright, has challenging carer responsibilities. She recently said to me: "The more gloomy things there are in one direction in my life, the more actively I seek joy in other areas. Not an excited sort of joy, but a quiet, smile-to-yourself sort. My indoor windowsill garden is joy for me at the moment."

Some scholars argue that joy has become increasingly absent in modern life.[20] I hope the lists and activities in this chapter will help you start to reclaim it.

Recapture Your Childhood Joys

Look back to when you were a child and list the five activities that brought you the most joy: for example, riding your bike, making up games to play, or perhaps splashing about in a paddling pool.

1

2

3

4

5

Take Action

What is a source of childhood joy you could bring back into your life now? Where and when will you try this?

Cherish Joyful Memories

We can savor joyful times in our past as well as feel joy in the present. List 10 moments you've experienced joy, whether recently or in the past. This might be a time you were able to dance freely and unselfconsciously, when your sports team won an important match, playing with a young child, making music, or a special time with friends. Only you know what brings you joy!

1

2

3

4

5

6

7

8

9

10

Pick one of the examples from your list and visualize yourself back in that moment. Take 10 minutes to relive that time in your mind: what was the location and context and what could you see, hear, and smell? Let your mind wander freely through the details. Repeat this once or twice a day for the next week.[21]

Reflection

How does it feel to reflect on and savor a past joyful experience? Were you able to rekindle a little of that joyful feeling? How could you savor joys you've experienced more regularly?

Your Joyful People

List the 10 people in your life with whom you share the most joyful moments.

1

2

3

4

5

Take Action

Now that you've identified your joyful people, consider when and how you keep in touch with them. When will you see them next?

Joy Spotting

Studies have shown that we can get an uplift from seeing another person's joy, whether it's someone we know or a stranger. It's called positive empathy![22] Over the next week, look out for small moments of joy happening to others around you. Aim to spot at least one moment each day.

Day	Who	What Was the Joyful Moment?
Monday		
Tuesday		
Wednesday		
Thursday		
Friday		
Saturday		
Sunday		

Reflection

How do you feel when you see another's joy? Do you experience a moment of joy at their joy, or do you feel a little envious? Try thinking from the other person's perspective and imagine how they're feeling, to help you feel some of their joy.

Spread a Little Joy

Not only does doing something kind for others boost their happiness, but it can also boost your own.[23] List 10 ways you could spread a little joy, then tick them off as you complete them.

The ways you give others joy could be new ideas or things you've done in the past—perhaps sending a thoughtful card or inspiring picture or quote, making someone a treat, or just ringing them for a chat to share something uplifting.

1 _____ ☐

2 _____ ☐

3 _____ ☐

4 _____ ☐

5 _____ ☐

6 _____ ☐

7 _____ ☐

8 _____ ☐

9 _____ ☐

10 _____ ☐

Reflection

Look back over the list of ways you've spread joy—how does it feel when you give joy to other people?

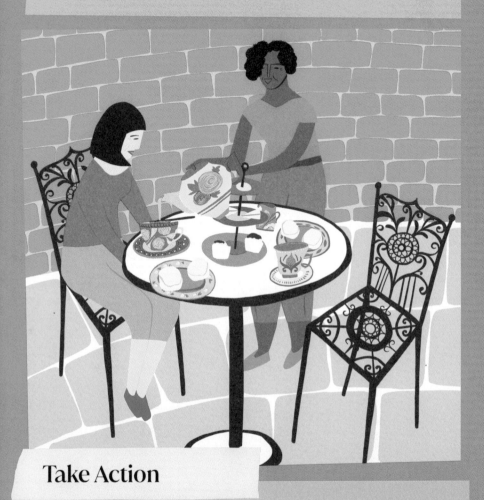

Take Action

- Think of someone in your life who might need a little joy right now, then pick something from your list to bring them a moment of joy, however small. When and how will you do this?

- Who else could you spread a little joy to?

Create a Joy Playlist

List 10 songs, pieces of music, or soundscapes that you find joyful. Put one of these on whenever you need a jolt of joy—you could even dance!

1 _____

2 _____

3 _____

4 _____

5 _____

6 _____

7 _____

8 _____

9 _____

10 _____

Create a Joy Watchlist

Create or bookmark 10 video clips or movies that help you feel uplifted and joyful, then list them below.

1

2

3

4

5

6

7

8

9

10

Take Action

Pick one of the clips or movies on your list to watch this week!

Build Joyful Moments into Your Day

Experiencing small moments of joy throughout the course of the day not only feels good, but can do us good, too. It can also help us persist with challenging tasks and cope with difficulties. List 10 ways you could include small, joyful moments in your daily routine. Tick them off when you've tried each one.

1 ☐
2 ☐
3 ☐
4 ☐
5 ☐
6 ☐
7 ☐
8 ☐
9 ☐
10 ☐

Helpful Hint

A joyful moment might be getting outside for a walk or bike ride, listening to a joyful tune, having a dance, noticing nature, enjoying your favorite dish, or perhaps phoning a joyful friend.

Take Action

- When and how will you incorporate your joyful moments regularly into your days?

- Look back at your lists for *Three Good Things* (pages 18–19) and *A Week of Good Things* (pages 20–21). Pick out any everyday moments of joy from what you've noted there that you could experience even more often.

Peace

For many of us, life today is very busy—we rush from one meeting to the next, or one task or chore to another, with very little space in between. More human doings than human beings! It's not surprising that we can feel overloaded or overwhelmed. In addition to this, our busy minds are racing with thoughts and worries, so it's no wonder many of us regularly feel stressed.

Learning to create small moments of calm or serenity in our day not only gives our minds and bodies a restorative mini-break, but it can also help us feel a bit more in control, which in itself is good for our psychological well-being.[24] Plus, sometimes it's in these timeouts or pauses that creative ideas pop into our mind!

Even a short pause when we notice our minds running away with worries or to-do lists, or if we're feeling overwhelmed, can help us shift how we feel, so we are better able to cope. For example, pausing and taking a slow breath or two can help us take a step back from the situation and make better choices, helping us to manage our thinking and reactions. Indeed, this is a first step toward the practice of mindfulness—when, with intention and practice, we learn to notice how we're feeling or where our mind is and, without judging or getting caught up in that, we kindly and deliberately bring our attention back to a more neutral point of focus such as our breath. There is strong evidence that the regular practice of mindfulness can significantly benefit our psychological well-being.[25]

Proactively punctuating each day or week with peaceful pauses helps us rest and restore. The activities that we find restful may vary—for some, these will be active like walking or exercise; for others, it might be reading, listening to music, or being in nature, or a mix of the two. A recent largescale study found that people who had paused to rest in some way in the previous 24 hours were more likely to feel happy the next day than people who felt they needed rest and got less rest than others.[26]

Pockets of Peace at Home

Our homes can be a haven, but they are often busy, with lots going on, and shared with other people. So, it can be beneficial to create a "pocket of peace" for when we need it.

How could you create a pocket of peace at home? It could be a physical space, such as a quiet corner for reading or looking at the view, or your bedroom or bathroom, or even a practice such as listening to some calming sounds on headphones. List five ways you could create a pocket of peace for yourself wherever you live:

1 _____

2 _____

3 _____

4 _____

5 _____

Reflection

When will you carve out some time to be nurtured by your personal pocket of peace?

Peaceful Pauses

Punctuating our day with focused moments of peace, even as short as a minute, can help us feel calmer and a little more in control. They can even help us be more productive and are great to take between back-to-back tasks, calls, and meetings.

Have a go at some of the peaceful pauses below over the next few days. Try each one for a minute and tick them off once you've tried them:

Look up at the sky
Really notice what you can see—colours, shapes, movement of the clouds, birds in flight. What else can you see?

Focus on your feet
Take your attention to your feet. Notice which parts of each foot touch the floor. What different temperatures or sensations can you feel? Feel how your feet are supported by the ground or floor. Send your breath to your feet, as if you are breathing in and out through the ground.

Listen to the sounds around you
What different sounds can you hear, from the loudest to the quietest? Start with those farthest away and gradually notice the sounds closer to where you are. Don't get caught up in labeling or judging what you hear—just listen. Notice how the sounds change over the course of a minute.

Practice 3 x 3 breathing

Sit or stand with your feet on the ground. Now breathe in slowly to the count of three and out to the count of three, then gently hold your breath for a count of three. Repeat the cycle for a minute.

Color spot

Pick a color, say green, yellow, or red, and then look carefully around you. Look for all the places where you can see that color, in all its different shades.

Reflection

After each peaceful pause you take, notice how you feel. How can you build some peaceful pauses into your day?

Helpful Hints

- Set a gentle alarm to remind you to take a peaceful pause.

- Try each of the peaceful pauses a few times until you get the hang of them.

- When you can, try slowly increasing the amount of time you spend in each moment once you've had more practice.

Peaceful Time Travel

Think back to five different times in the past when you've felt calm and at peace, then list them below.

1 _____

2 _____

3 _____

4 _____

5 _____

For each one in turn, take a few moments to remember where you were and what you were doing and feeling. What made the place or time calming and peaceful for you?

Helpful Hints

- Next time you feel stressed or overwhelmed, pick one time from your list and imagine being back there in as much detail as you can—think about the surroundings, sounds, smells, how the air feels on your skin, what you are doing, how peaceful and calm you are feeling. Breathe that in.

- You could keep photographs of your peaceful times or places on your phone or computer to look at when you need to.

Take Action

- Is there a peaceful location locally you could walk to? When will you do this?

- Find 10 songs, pieces of music, or soundscapes (such as the sea or birdsong) that you find calming. Create a playlist of these on your phone to listen to whenever you need a peaceful moment. They can be great to listen to on a journey!

Nature Spotting

Being in or close to nature has been shown to reduce stress, help us feel happier, and boost well-being.[27] Even if you live in a town or city, nature can be found everywhere—for example, trees or a pond in the park, a lovely window box, fungi or spring flowers growing from a wall, or birds flying in the sky!

Explore your local area and spot 10 different pockets of nature. Then note them down here:

1

2

3

4

5

6

7

8

9

10

Helpful Hint

Take pictures of what you see and use these as a screensaver or to reflect on.

Nature Watch

Studies have shown[28] that looking at nature videos can help to reduce stress and boredom and make us feel calmer and happier.

Create a peaceful nature watchlist of 10 short video clips that you find calming, then list them here:

1 _____

2 _____

3 _____

4 _____

5 _____

6 _____

7 _____

8 _____

9 _____

10 _____

Helpful Hints

- Ask your friends for video clips that they've found peaceful and share one or more of yours with them.

- Try watching one of the videos you've listed to help you switch off after work, school, or college.

Curiosity

Our curiosity is sparked when we encounter something new—it grabs our attention and interest, and we find ourselves wanting to find out more. Curiosity drives our motivation to seek out new information or uncertain or novel experiences, and then learn from these,[29] creating a feel-good reaction in our brain when we do.[30] In this way, our curiosity provides fuel for creativity and problem-solving, too.

While children are naturally curious, we tend to become less so as adults. However, research has shown that curiosity predicts healthier, happier aging[31]—so it's worth the effort to maintain and cultivate it! We can get curious to know and find out more about other people or the world around us, to gain knowledge and learn about specific topics or skills, and to understand ourselves better.

There's ease in the familiar: doing what we know or we like, connecting with the same people, eating the same food, or listening to the same types of music. Seeking out or encountering something new can be uncomfortable, even a bit scary. Getting curious instead of fearful can help us approach rather than avoid new situations or people. It helps us to explore and discover, literally expanding our world and our horizons.

Of course, if we're trying something for the first time, it can feel uncomfortable and take more conscious effort. We may be frustrated because we aren't likely to be as instantly good at it as we'd perhaps like to be. Accepting this as part of the process of trying things and learning helps us stay with what's new and expand our knowledge and skills. So, instead of saying to yourself "I'm no good at this" or "I don't know if I like this," and sticking to what's familar, try adding "yet" to your self-talk—"I'm no good at this... yet" or "I don't know if I like this... yet."[32]

Start to cultivate your curiosity with the lists and activities in this chapter—and see what you find out!

What Would You Love to Learn?

What are five things you'd like to learn more about? (For me, this is currently drawing, speaking basic Greek, cooking a different cuisine, learning to kayak, and mastering DIY.)

1
2
3
4
5

Take Action

- Pick one of the things on your list and plan how, when, and where you'll get started.

- Look around you and find five everyday objects, such as a fork, cup, or clock. Now get curious and find out something you didn't know about each one—how it was first designed or developed, how it is made, or how it was used historically or by different cultures. What have you learned that surprised you?

Break Out of Your Routines

Being flexible can boost our creativity and resilience, as well as our curiosity, yet we often live much of our life on autopilot, following the same routines without thinking.

A regular routine might be the route you usually take to work, school, or college; the grocery store you go to; what you eat for breakfast or lunch; your morning or nighttime routine; or the news channel you watch or listen to most often. List five of your regular routines:

1 ☐

2 ☐

3 ☐

4 ☐

5 ☐

Once you've listed your routines, think of something you could do to change each one. For example, for a journey you routinely take to work, try changing the route or mode of transport, or simply look up or around you more rather than focusing on your phone or the thoughts in your mind. Or, if you always have coffee and toast for breakfast, try something new. Tick off each routine once you've tried something new. Give yourself a pat on the back when you have. It's not easy!

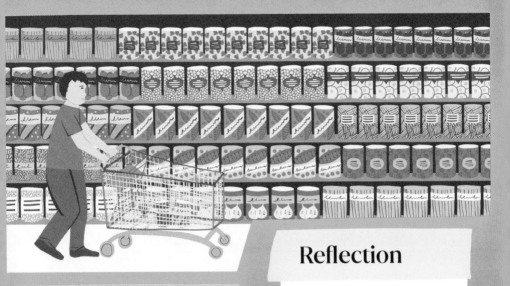

Reflection

Keep an open mind. See what you notice and how it feels to break out of your routine.

Helpful Hint

Remember that it takes a bit more effort and also courage to try something new. Try your new way a few times to see what you can take from the experience.

Get Curious About Others

Curiosity is important for our connections with others. As psychologist and curiosity expert Todd Kashden says: "Being interested is more important in cultivating and maintaining relationships than being interesting."

Get started

Over the next week, get curious when you connect with others—try asking people some simple open questions. The three below are a good starting point. Tick off the questions when you've asked them, using a tick for each person you asked:

What's something you most love doing in your spare time and what do you love about it?

What's your favorite place locally and what does it mean to you?

What's your favorite ever book or movie and what makes it stand out for you?

Reflection

How did getting curious about others in this way feel? What did you notice as a result—about yourself, the other person/people, and your connection with them? What did you learn?

Helpful Hint

Really listen to and take an interest in each of the other person's answers, perhaps asking a few more questions about it. Only share your thoughts once you've explored their answers.

Ask playful and curious questions

It's easy to make assumptions or just talk about the same old things, but people are full of surprises, whether they're people you know well or new people you meet. It can be fun to try asking some different, playful, curious questions and see what you find out! Tick off the ones you've tried asking.

What was your favorite toy or game as a child? What did you love about it? ☐

What's the kindest thing someone has ever done for you? ☐

What's the kindest thing you've ever done? ☐

If you could do any job in the world, what would you do and why? ☐

Which characters from history, movies, or fiction would you like to invite to dinner and why? ☐

If you could try living in a new country for three months, where would you choose and why? ☐

What superpower would you like to have in order to make a difference in the world? How would you use it? ☐

Take Action

When, where, and with whom will you give this activity a try?

Get Curious About Nature

Nature can be a constant source of wonder and it's all around us if we look, even in towns and cities. It can be a source of calm, too.

Head outdoors to a local park, your street, or backyard and pick a small area (roughly a few feet square—there's no need to be precise). Even a window box or patch of ground with plants will do. Get curious about what's there and ask the following questions:

- What different colors, textures, and shapes can you see in your chosen area?

- What plants and insects are there?

- Do you know the names of everything you can see?

- Can you learn more about one of the plants or insects that you've spotted?

List (or even sketch) what you saw and found out below:

1

2

3

4

5

6

7

8

9

10

Wants and Whys

We often get an instant happiness boost when we buy something new, but the feeling soon subsides and then we want the next new thing. Psychologists and economists call this the "hedonic treadmill." It doesn't lead to longer-term happiness or fulfillment and may not be good for our pockets or the planet either!

We may want something new because we like the enjoyable distraction of shopping, we're bored, or we want to feel better about ourselves, rather than because we need it. If we can understand what's really behind our wants, we are more likely to find other ways to fulfill our underlying needs.

So, when you find yourself wanting to buy something new (perhaps a new outfit or gadget), get curious about what's actually behind this. If we can understand what's really behind our wants, we can try to find more fulfilling ways to meet our underlying needs—and that's good for helping to make us happier and the planet healthier.

Identify your why

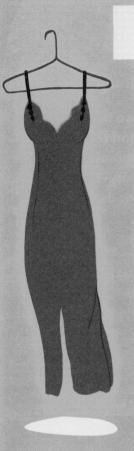

First, ask yourself (and note your reply):
What would I like to buy right now?:

_____

Now ask yourself (and note your replies):
Why do I want this?

_____

Then ask, "Why's that?" to that response

_____

Then ask, "Why's that?" again to that response

_____

And again ask, "Why's that?"

_____

Keep going until you don't have any more answers to "Why's that?"

Now think creatively about other ways you could potentially meet your underlying want or need. List your ideas below:

1 _____

2 _____

3 _____

Pride

Accepting and feeling good about ourselves creates a firm foundation for well-being.[33] Rather than comparing ourselves to others, focusing on what we're not, or dwelling on our mistakes and failures, there are always things we can be proud of if we learn to pay some attention to them.

For many of us, feeling good about ourselves doesn't come naturally. It may not be culturally or socially acceptable, as is reinforced by sayings such as "Pride comes before a fall." The role of social media in our lives has made it so much more likely that we compare ourselves to what we perceive others to be like, and then feel lacking as a result. Or we feel we must present an image that isn't the real us. Both of which can significantly undermine our happiness.

Accepting ourselves and feeling pride isn't about seeing ourselves as better than others, but rather understanding that each of us has a unique blend of strengths, talents, and weaker areas, and can learn how to manage and make the most of these.

In the last two decades, there has been a growing science of strengths. Our strengths are positive qualities that are us at our natural best—qualities which feel authentic, we are drawn to using, and that we find energizing. Science shows that when we understand our strengths and find ways to use and develop these, it can help us to feel happier, more confident, and perform better, and it can boost our resilience too.[34] This doesn't mean ignoring weaker areas, but putting these more into perspective and making the most of what we naturally do well.

How we treat ourselves when we make mistakes also matters. Research shows that if we recognize that everyone fails or messes up at times and learn to cultivate a compassionate inner coach, rather than a harsh critic, we feel happier, are less likely to be depressed or anxious, and more motivated to improve, learn, and grow.[35]

In this chapter, there are lists and activities to try that will help you explore and focus on the best of you and suggestions for some simple ways to begin developing more self-compassion.

You At Your Best

Bring to mind a time when you were proud of yourself or when you felt energized or at your natural best. This doesn't need to be anything huge or even the very best time. It could be something like arranging a treat for a friend, helping someone out, or perhaps overcoming a challenge. It can be something recent or in the past. It doesn't need to be when other people said you performed well. What matters most is, it was a time that you felt proud of you.

Note your example below:

Now reflect on what the situation was, what you did, and what happened as a result. What specifically made you proud of yourself? Think about this in as much detail as possible. List at least three strengths, skills, or talents you used in this situation.

1

2

3

4

5

Take Action

Pick one of the strengths you identified and find a way to use it more or in a new way over the next week. Think about where and when you will do this.

Catch Yourself Doing Something Right

Train your brain to notice good things about you and what you do! Each evening for the next week, reflect on your day. List three things you did that pleased you about you. These can be tiny—for example, something small you did well, a moment of kindness to others or yourself, a strength you used, something you learned or noticed that gave you a moment of pride, or even something you were pleased that you *didn't* do!

Monday

1
2
3

Tuesday

1
2
3

Wednesday

1
2
3

Thursday

1
2
3

Friday

1
2
3

Saturday

1
2
3

Sunday

1
2
3

Reflection

Looking back over the lists from this week, what do you notice? How does it make you feel?

Explore Your Strengths:
Take a Survey

Psychologists have developed a range of different surveys to help people discover and explore their strengths. One of the most widely used is the VIA Survey of Character Strengths. There's a free version that has been taken by millions of people around the world. The survey takes around 15 minutes to complete. You can find it here: https://www.viacharacter.org (there are versions for different languages).

You will receive a listing of 24 character strengths in rank order, starting from the strongest. This is your personal profile. All 24 character strengths are positive and we can draw on any of them, depending on the situation, but some will be more natural and authentic for us.

Reflect on the top five or so strengths in your ranking:

- Do these strengths feel like the real you (rather than what you think you should be like)?

- Are these strengths energizing and effortless for you, and do you enjoy using them?

Based on your reflections, list below the five strengths that you feel are most authentically you. These are your "signature strengths":

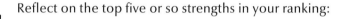

1

2

3

4

5

Over the next week or so start to notice when, where, and how you are using your signature strengths and how you feel when you do.

Explore Your Strengths: Ask Others

People you know will see strengths in you that perhaps you don't notice yourself. Pick three (or more) people you trust and who care about you, and ask them if they'd each share three strengths they see in you. Ideally, ask a mix of people—who know you in different capacities—such as a friend, family member, or colleague.

Capture their answers in the table below:

Name	Relationship to Me	Strengths They See in Me
_____ _____ _____	_____ _____ _____	1 _____ 2 _____ 3 _____
_____ _____ _____	_____ _____ _____	1 _____ 2 _____ 3 _____
_____ _____ _____	_____ _____ _____	1 _____ 2 _____ 3 _____
_____ _____ _____	_____ _____ _____	1 _____ 2 _____ 3 _____

Remember, only you can know what your strengths really are. What others see will be dependent on the context in which they know you and what's important to them. You will have many positive qualities and capabilities and learned many skills that others might identify. However, these might not be what you most enjoy using, find most energizing, and feel most "you" at your natural best.

Reflection

Now reflect on the strengths that people see in you:

- What are the common themes or differences among the strengths?

- Are these similar or different to your signature strengths (see page 67)?

- Are there any strengths you hadn't paid attention to in yourself? Are these strengths you find energizing?

- What do you notice about how you use your strengths in different contexts? Are there areas you could use any of your strengths more?

Put Your Strengths into Action

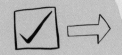

Now that you've explored your strengths in various different ways, it's time to put them into action! Here are some ideas to get you started.

Tackle your to-do list

In the table below, list five tasks on your to-do list that are a challenge in some way. For each task identify one of your signature strengths (see page 67) that you can use in tackling it. When you are doing the task, consciously focus on applying that strength to help you. Tick each task off the list once you've completed it.

Task	Strength I Used?	
1		☐
2		☐
3		☐
4		☐
5		☐

Use a strength in a new way

Pick one strength and identify a way you can use it more or differently over the next week. In a study,[36] when people did this each day for a week, they were less likely to feel down up to six months later.

The strength I'll use more/differently this week is:

How:

Where:

When:

Strengthen your social connections

Pick one of your VIA signature strengths (see page 67) and use it to help you nurture your connection with another person. For example, you might use "Appreciation of Beauty and Excellence" to let them know what you really value in them or "Bravery" to strike up a conversation with someone new. List the name of the person and then tick off the strength when you've used it.

Name of Person	Strength I Will Use and How	
1		☐
2		☐
3		☐

Change Your Inner Critic into a Wise Coach

Many of us have a harsh inner critic. We are tougher on and more critical of ourselves than we are of others. Although the intention of our inner critic is to help us to be better, it generally has the opposite effect. It makes us feel bad about ourselves, making us less happy and confident, and more stressed, reducing our ability to learn from mistakes and grow.

Think back to a time you messed up or failed in some way.
What did you say to yourself? Note it here:

_____

_____

How did you say it (tone of voice, etc.)?:

_____

_____

Were you tougher or harsher with yourself than you'd be with a good friend who messed up or failed in a similar way?

_____

_____

Cultivating a wise inner coach instead of our harsh inner critic doesn't mean we shy away from mistakes and failure. Instead, by being kinder, a wise inner coach helps us look at and learn from these and so we are more likely to improve. A coach recognizes that we feel bad, reminds us that everyone messes up sometimes, and helps us to move forward constructively, not get stuck on beating ourselves up.[37]

Now write down what a wise inner coach would say in response to the mistake or failure you identified opposite and also how they'd say it. For example: *"I can see you're upset about that error, that's natural. We all make mistakes. What can you take from this to help you next time?"*

My inner coach would say:

_____

_____

How would they say it (tone of voice, etc.)?:

_____

_____

Self-Compassionate Reminders

When you feel frustrated with yourself, it can be helpful to have a few compassionate phrases you can think or say out loud. Perhaps try the examples given here or write your own.

Pick one phrase at a time to try out next time you feel yourself getting annoyed or upset with yourself. Find a way to remind yourself of it. You might try putting each one in a reminder on your phone or on sticky notes, keeping these in a place you can see them. Tick off the ones you've tried:

"I'm aiming to be real, not perfect."

Reflection

Which phrase or phrases worked well for you? What did you notice from this experiment?

Amusement

A friend of mine used to read a joke book before going into important exams as it helped her manage pre-exam nerves. This turned out to be a good strategy for her and may have had other benefits, too. As we explored in the Introduction, the experience of positive, pleasant emotions also helps us to see more options and be better at creative problem-solving— useful in exams! The benefits of laughter extend beyond this. Genuine laughter not only feels good; it also boosts our pain thresholds[38] and shared laughter is thought to facilitate social bonding.[39] Indeed, research shows we laugh up to 30 times more when we are with others than when we are alone[40] and laughter can be highly contagious![41]

Laughter is a spontaneous, non-verbal expression. We laugh most with people we like and with whom we feel safe. When we share laughter with others, we feel closer to them and like them more.[42] It may even help us to deal with difficulties with each other.[43] These positive outcomes for our connections with others only occur if the topic of laughter is shared—laughing at someone who doesn't share the joke or finds it offensive will probably have a detrimental effect.

As well as finding things funny, having fun is good for us too and can also help nurture our connections with others. We know that play is important in childhood, but in our busy lives as grown-ups, it can be hard to make time to do things just for fun. Research shows, however, that play can also benefit adults, helping to reduce stress and boosting our creativity, as well as supporting our psychological and physical wellbeing.[44]

Laughter Lists

Think about the last time you really laughed, then answer the following questions:

Who were you with?

What was the situation?

What led to the laughter?

How do you feel remembering this time?

Who have you laughed with most over the course of your life? List their names here:

1

2

3

4

5

Consider what it was about those relationships that enabled you to laugh a lot together?

Finding Time for Fun

Think about the last time you did something just for fun. When was it? What did you do and what enabled you to do it? Now list five to ten things you could do just for fun over the next couple of weeks.

1 _____

2 _____

3 _____

4 _____

5 _____

6 _____

7 _____

8 _____

9 _____

10 _____

Reflection

When and how will you make time for the fun things on your list? Visualize where you'll do them.

Take Action

Who can you share a fun time with in the next few weeks?
How can you make this happen?

Make Movement Fun

Not only does keeping active and moving feel good, but it is also important for our physical health. Don't worry if you're not sporty or dislike the gym—there are lots of ways to add more moments of movement to your day.

How about finding a video of fun dance moves and giving them a go; doing some gardening; going for a brisk walk and talk with a friend; making housework fun by doing it to upbeat music; and even walking on the spot at home while watching your favorite comedy show! List five to ten ways of being active that you enjoy.

1

2

3

4

5

6

7

8

9

10

Reflection

Look back over your list of fun ways to move more and think about the following:

- Sitting for long periods of time is bad for our health. How can you punctuate your sitting with small moments of movement each day? Even a minute or two can make a difference!

- How can you ensure you make time for regular physical activities that you enjoy?

Visualize when and where you'll do these (and how you could get around what might get in the way).

Spread Some Laughter: Joke Swap

Find five jokes you find funny (and, of course, aren't offensive). Pick one and share it with a friend you haven't already told it to. Ask them to share one of their favorite jokes with you. Repeat with the other jokes (and other friends). Tick off each one once you've shared it.

1 ☐

2 ☐

3 ☐

4 ☐

5 ☐

Helpful Hint

Search for "Christmas cracker jokes" on the Internet to find some very cheesy jokes!

Comedy Checklist

Think of five of your all-time favorite comedy shows, movies, or clips, then list them below.

1
2
3
4
5

Over the next few weeks, make time to rewatch one or more of these and really savor the amusement you feel. (It can be a great thing to do if you are feeling a little down and/or to do with a friend.)

Take Action

Why not share your comedy checklist with friends or family and ask people to share their favorites with you? Perhaps you could find an opportunity to watch some of these shows together?

Awe

The experience of awe can be uplifting and inspiring. It takes us out of ourselves and can have positive benefits as a result, both for us and others. Awe, that natural sense of "wow" and wonder, can feel mysterious. Something we experience when we encounter a greatness or vastness that we can't explain or which causes us to question, adjust, or expand our understanding of the world.[45]

When we think of our own experiences of awe, nature often comes to mind, such as panoramic views, sky-high mountains, or sparkling, bright white, snowy landscapes, but it can also be found in urban contexts. We can evoke awe in everyday life by encountering things outside of our normal range of expectations or experience. We may experience awe firsthand, or through movies, videos, or stories, or by recalling a memory. Remembering the first time I visited New York and saw the Manhattan skyline at night come into view, as my taxi sped along the expressway from the airport, still takes my breath away.

Awe can also be found through seeing exemplary performance or goodness in others and we can harness what we see to inspire us in our daily lives. It can be found in the beauty that surrounds us if we pause to look and listen, be that tiny flowers, birdsong, tall trees in a local park, or works of art or music.

While the scientific study of awe is still relatively young, resesarch suggests that it can reduce stress[46] and rumination (churning over worries and thoughts), boost our mood, increase life satisfaction and our sense of time, and help us to feel more connected to other people. It can also induce a sense of spirituality and might even make us less materialistic.[47]

Awe momentarily blurs the boundary between ourselves and the world around us and helps us put things into perspective. Experiencing awe reduces self-focus, boosts humility,[48] and research shows that it also makes us more likely to be kind and help others.[49]

Awesome Beauty

Works of art, music, or other objects of beauty can uplift and inspire us. They can help us transcend the nitty-gritty or worries of our daily lives, even if just for a moment.

Think about it—what do you find truly beautiful? It could be a painting or sculpture you love, a piece of music you find transcendent, a specific bird or flower, or an exquisite historical artifact. List five things you find beautiful below:

1 _____

2 _____

3 _____

4 _____

5 _____

Take Action

- Capture pictures of your five awesome things and look at them whenever you need a moment of uplift or inspiration.

- Pick one of the pictures of your things and spend a few minutes really focusing on it and taking it in. Notice any feelings, thoughts, or ideas that arise in you.

Awe in Nature

Nature is a never-ending source of awe—amazing landscapes, the great vastness of seas and deserts, natural phenomena such as the Northern Lights, the huge distances to the stars we see in the sky, or the ingenuity of wildlife perfectly adapted to its environment.

Which examples from the natural world fill you with awe or wonder? Note these down. Bring each one to mind in turn and reflect on what specifically is awe-inspiring for you.

Example from Nature	What Makes This Inspiring?
1	
2	
3	
4	
5	
6	
7	
8	
9	
10	

Reflection

How could thinking about or looking at images of these amazing and awe-inspiring aspects of the natural world help put your worries into perspective?

Take Action

Create a folder on your phone or laptop of images or videos of the examples of awe-inspiring nature you listed.

Local Awe Walks

Studies have found[50] that going for walks where we purposefully try to notice things that inspire awe in us not only feels good and distracts us from our own worries, but can also make us more likely to help others.

Have a go! Over the next six to eight weeks, at least once a week, go for a 15-minute walk during which you focus on spotting things that inspire a sense of awe and wonder in you. Try to look as if you're seeing things for the first time. Note down 10 things you spot during your walks that inspire awe in you in some way:

1 _____

2 _____

3 _____

4 _____

5 _____

6 _____

7 _____

8 _____

9 _____

10 _____

Helpful Hint

It doesn't matter if the walk is in the countryside, a local park, or an urban area. There are always things that inspire awe if we look for wonder in the world—for example, the very tallest trees or tiniest fragile plants pushing through hard earth or a crack in the ground; the dramatic beauty of a sunset; the craftsmanship on an old building or the design of a modern one; the engineering feat of a bridge or tunnel; a panoramic view; or the sheer resilience of humans or nature.

Take Action

Take photos of the awesome things you spotted and create a portfolio or share them with friends.

Reflection

How did taking awe walks feel for you?

Amazing Humans

Human beings can be a source of awe and wonder. As a species, we've been amazingly innovative and creative through history. There are countless extraordinary examples: scientific discoveries, sporting or artistic achievements, and people who have shown selfless leadership or courage.

List 10 feats of amazing human innovation or achievement. What is it about these that inspire you?

Innovation or Achievement	What Makes This Inspiring?
1	
2	
3	
4	
5	
6	
7	
8	
9	
10	

Take Action

Pick one innovation or achievement from your list and research the story behind it. Find out how the people involved persevered and overcame the inevitable struggles and challenges along the way.

Reflection

What inspiration can you take from this exercise to help you as you pursue a goal that matters to you or deal with a current challenge?

Ordinary Heroes

Mother Teresa is reported to have said: "Not all of us can do great things, but we can all do small things with great love."

Inspiration is not only found in elite performance, but also in those around us or who we watch, or read or hear about—people who overcome trauma, perform acts of heroism, get out of their comfort zone to take on a challenge, or make something beautiful out of seemingly nothing.

It can also be found in the small things people do to help others or contribute to their communities, day in and day out.

Over the next two weeks, look for the local heroes in your own community and scan the news and other media sources for extraordinary, inspiring acts by ordinary people. List five to ten of these here:

1 _____

2 _____

3 _____

4 _____

5 _____

6 _____

7 _____

8 _____

9 _____

10 _____

Reflection

What is it about the examples on your list that you find most inspiring? How could you use this in your own life?

Love

Happiness is social. Whether you're an introvert or extrovert, experiencing positive connections with others is the most important ingredient for living a happier life.[51] In fact, feeling lonely can damage both our psychological and physical health.[52]

Our close relationships matter most—having people we trust and care about and who care about us is an essential component of well-being. We need people we can share our good news with and who are there for us when we have difficulties, and for whom we do the same.[53] Our wider social connections and even momentary interactions in our communities also make a difference.

The ancient Greeks had words for different types of love, such as: *agápē* (a universal, unconditional form of love for everyone, including strangers, and encompassing compassion, empathy, and kindness); *philía* (deep friendship); *storgē* (family love); and *éros* and *pragma* (romantic and committed love, respectively). Dr. Barbara Fredrickson, a leading emotions scientist, argues that at its core, love should be considered "a pleasant and momentary experience of connection with another person (or persons)." Our deeper, stronger connections result from an accumulation of such moments.[54]

Research also shows that our mood states are contagious, literally rippling out through our social networks (and vice versa).[55] When we share a pleasant emotional moment with someone else, the beneficial broaden-and-build effect we explored in the Introduction is amplified for each person via the hormone and neurotransmitter oxytocin. Oxytocin calms us down and attunes us more to the other person, increasing the likelihood of further shared positive emotions.[56] Studies show[57] there are lots of small things we can do to foster shared moments of pleasant or positive connection and nurture and strengthen our close relationships.

Acts of kindness and appreciation are great for nuturing connection. They're like a "social glue" that helps build and maintain our relationships and communities. They can also be catching. If someone witnesses us doing something kind or thanking another person, they're more likely to help others too.[58] Being kind is also a great way to boost happiness—it can take our minds off our own worries and give both us and the recipient of our kindness a feel-good boost.[59] There are many ways to be kind, including: smiling or being complimentary; giving time, things, or money; and being appreciative.

Your Nearest and Dearest

Who are five people you feel close to and support you when you need it? List their names below and note down one thing you really appreciate about each of them.

Name	What I Appreciate About This Person
1	
2	
3	
4	
5	

Reflection

It's important to let the people closest to you know that you value and appreciate them, as they can often be the ones we take for granted! How can you let the people on your list know what you appreciate about them and what they do for you?

Thank You Plus Plus

Most of us know the importance of thanking people when they've done something kind for us.[60] We can amplify our thanks by adding a couple of simple extra details: being specific about the positive impact on us of what the person did and highlighting a positive quality we observed in them as a result.

Here's an everyday example: *"Thanks for helping me prepare the meal—that really helped reduce the pressure on me. You are a really considerate friend."*

For the people you listed for *Your Nearest and Dearest* (see page 101), think of something each has done for you, then note below the positive impact that had on you and the quality in them you experienced as a result.

Name	Positive Impact	Positive Quality
1		
2		
3		
4		
5		

Take Action

- Try 'Thank you plus plus' in your everyday interactions and see what you notice.

- Send a message or card to say thank you to the people on your list and tell them the impact they've had for you. Even better, say it to them in person!

Take an Interest in Their Good Stuff

We often think that being there for other people when they are having a bad time is the most important thing in our relationships and, of course, this does matter. However, studies show[61] that how we respond to the good news they share also matters—a lot!

Think back to a couple of recent examples of someone sharing something good with you. It could be big, like a new job or relationship, or small, such as having a fun night out, learning a new skill, or enjoying a movie or gig. Which of the responses below best reflects how you responded in both your examples?

a) "That's great," and then you quickly moved on to another topic.

b) "That's great," and then you shared something similar for you.

c) "Sounds good, but have you thought about...?"
   [you highlighted a risk or worry].

d) "That's great," followed by a few questions to find out more.

Now note down which type of response (a, b, c, or d) you used in both your examples:

Person's Name and the Good Thing They Shared	Your Response Type
1	
2	

In the studies, the only style of responding that strengthened the relationship was taking an active interest in the other person's piece of good news, by asking a few questions and listening to their responses BEFORE sharing any of our own news or opinions or pointing out any risks or worries! All it takes is a few open and interested questions.

Here's an example. If someone shares that they had a great time out last night, you might ask, in a friendly way: "Where did you go?", "Who did you go with?", and "What was it that you most enjoyed about the night?"

Take Action

Over the next few days, listen out for people sharing a piece of good news with you and try asking a few interested questions. Note below three things you noticed as a result of doing this:

1
2
3

Whole Body Listening

One of the most important skills for building and nurturing our relationships is listening well—really well! Yet we are often multitasking on our phones or other devices, or getting caught up with our own thoughts of what to say in response.

A time I felt really listened to

Think back to a time when you felt really listened to. How did that feel and how did you feel about the other person as a result? What did they do that helped you feel listened to? List your thoughts below:

1

2

3

4

5

How do I respond in conversations?

Think back to a recent conversation you had with someone—perhaps a time when they were sharing something important for them. Now, being honest, which of the following did you do?

Gave them my fully focused attention.

Didn't multitask and put my phone away.

Noticed their body language. ☐

Signalled that I was listening (ie. by nodding my head or saying "Yes" or "Uhhuh"). ☐

Only spoke when they had finished. ☐

Reflected back the key things they communicated (with their words, tone, and body language) to check if that was right. ☐

Asked if they wanted to hear my thoughts and ideas, rather than launching straight into my response. ☐

Listened more than I spoke (there's a reason we have two ears and two eyes and only one mouth)! ☐

Take Action

Listening well is a skill we can learn. Pick one or two of the points in the checklist you didn't do, and over the next week practice those in conversations you have. It may feel awkward at first, but you'll get the hang of it. Notice the impact listening well has on the other person and your connection with them. Note what you tried out and noticed:

1

2

3

4

5

Strengths Priming

Our interactions with others aren't always easy. We might find some people difficult or need to raise a tricky issue with someone we care about. It's easy to focus on what we don't like about the people we find difficult, but they will also have some positive qualities.

Reflecting on a person's strengths or positive qualities just before we connect with them can help moderate how we interact and reduce our anxiety before we do, making a positive, constructive outcome more likely.

List a few people that you find difficult (or with whom you need to have a difficult conversation). Note some positive qualities that they have:

Name of Person	Person's Positive Qualities
1	
2	
3	

How can you remind yourself to bring their strengths to mind ahead of connecting with them?

Reflection

If you are finding someone difficult, try "standing in their shoes" and seeing the situation from their perspective. Could you find a way together to combine your strengths to resolve the issue?

Kindness Ripple Day

Acts of kindness are contagious. If someone is on the receiving end of kindness, they are more likely to be kind themselves. Even observing an act of kindness increases the likelihood that we'll then be kind to someone else.

Pick a day to create a ripple of kindness. Find five ways to be kind, in addition to what you'd normally do. For example, leave a nice note or treat for someone to find; pay someone a compliment; pay-it-forward in a coffee shop; offer to help someone who is stressed or struggling; or check in on an elderly neighbor.

My five extra acts of kindness were:

1 _____

2 _____

3 _____

4 _____

5 _____

Notice how you feel having done your extra acts of kindness.

Take Action

In a famous psychology study,[62] people who created a kindness ripple day for one day a week for six weeks experienced a happiness boost. Why not have a kindness day each week for the next six weeks. Try varying the acts of kindness you do to enhance the happiness boost.

Sustainable Giving

Being kind and helping others is good for happiness—both our own and that of others. To be a long-term giver, however, we need to find ways to do this that we can sustain. The psychologist Adam Grant calls this being "other-ish"—neither completely selfless, yet not selfish.

Enjoy giving

Think about which ways of helping or giving to others you most enjoy and how you could use your strengths in kind ways? List a few here:

1

2

3

4

5

How can you help or give to others regularly?

Five-minute favors

It can be tricky to help others if we're busy or don't have much spare time, but even something quick can make a difference. Think about the different ways you could help or be kind that take five minutes or less. For example, you could make a quick call to check in on someone; send an article or link that someone might find helpful; highlight what someone is doing well; or create a useful connection between people you know.

1

2

3

4

5

Take Action

Could you find a few minutes each day to do a five-minute favor for someone?

Hope

Hope is an emotion that often arises when we face difficulties or fear the worst. It enables us to feel that things can change for the better and creates the urge to draw on our capabilities and internal or external resources to take action to help improve things or move forward.[63] In this way, hope is active rather than just a wish that things can be better.

In a book about cultivating happiness, it's important to recognize that feeling happier doesn't mean we'll never feel unhappy. Life can have downs as well as ups. Everyone faces challenges and rough times. Importantly, the science of happiness and well-being doesn't just enable us to maintain feeling good; it can also give us a boost when we need it and may help us cope and have hope when we're finding things tough.[64] For example, Dr. Maria Sirois, a clinical psychologist who has worked with the terminally ill and their families, applies the research on feeling gratitude even on the darkest days as a result of illness, loss, or trauma. She advises that even on the worst days there will be a best moment—it doesn't matter if this is just the least bad one. Recalling a best (or least bad) moment each day before going to bed can help us cope.

What's known as active or adaptive coping is a source of resilience and hope when we are experiencing difficult times in our lives. Aligned with ideas from positive psychology and acceptance and commitment therapy, active coping involves acknowledging, not ignoring, how we're feeling in the midst of the difficulties we are experiencing *and also* taking action that could make our today or tomorrow slightly better. Indeed, doing something, rather than nothing, contributes to resilience, even if what we try is tiny. It can help us feel a little bit more in control, which is important for our well-being, especially when things are uncertain and challenging, and that sense of agency can help us see small glimmers of light or hope.[65] The ideas and activities throughout this book are a source of ideas to try.

Hope can also come through a better understanding of how we can support or undermine our own happiness through our habits and practices of thought. When our mind is stuck on churning over worries, inaccurate interpretations about what's happened, or catastrophizing—leaping to the worst-case scenario rather than what's most likely—it can compromise our resilience and contribute to us feeling worse. So, it can help to have a menu of tactics to try to help us shift or manage our thinking. Hope can also be found through other people and seeking or even offering help.

Find Things to Look Forward To

Finding things we're looking forward to and reflecting on them can give us a happiness boost and reduce worry.[66] Even if we're having a tough time, we can usually find something we can look forward to, however small that may be.

Try it. Think about your day tomorrow and identify three things you could look forward to? These can be simple or something bigger, but make sure they have a reasonable likelihood of happening. For example, a call with a friend, your favorite coffee, trying a new recipe, or spending 15 minutes in a hot bathtub at the end of the day.

Three things I'm looking forward to tomorrow are:

1

2

3

Now spend a few minutes imagining each of these in as much detail as you can—bring to mind what you'll see, hear, smell, and feel, and what you'll enjoy about them.

Helpful Hint

You can also use this visualization activity for things you're looking forward to further into the future, like a vacation, meeting up with friends, or an event you've got tickets for.

Resilient You

Spend some time reflecting on challenges and difficulties that you've experienced in the past and how you came through.

Dealing with challenges

List five things that helped you deal with these challenges or move on:

1

2

3

4

5

What did you learn about yourself?

List five helpful things you learned about yourself from going through these difficult times:

1

2

3

4

5

Reflection

Review these lists and then identify one thing you can draw on to help with a current challenge you may be facing.

Ask for Help When You Need It

Do you find it easier to help others than to ask for it for yourself? If your response is "yes," then you are not alone! Many of us don't like to ask for help in case others think poorly of us, or we don't want to burden people or feel we should know how or be able to cope. Yet asking for help is a sign of hope and resilience when we're struggling, want to learn something new, or simply need an extra pair of hands.

Asking for help builds connection. Neuroscience shows that helping others feels good,[67] so think of asking for help as giving someone the opportunity for a happiness boost. Feeling other people are there to support us (and vice versa) helps us feel we aren't alone in our struggles. Communities that help each other are stronger and happier, too.[68]

My immediate support network

List three people who you could turn to first for help when you are struggling:

1

2

3

Help to learn and grow

Think of something you wish to learn, advice that might be helpful, or a task you need a helping hand with. List three people you could ask:

1

3

2

Pick one person from this list—when and how will you ask them to help you?

Common Thinking Traps

Ever got annoyed with someone or upset at something, but found out later you'd got the wrong end of the stick? You might well have fallen into what's called a "thinking trap."

When something triggers an unpleasant emotional reaction in us, like anger, behind it is an instant instinctive interpretation about the situation (often why it happened or what might happen next). Not only does this drive what we feel in that moment, but also what we do as a result—which has knock-on consequences for us and others. This all happens so fast we often don't notice we've made an interpretation.

The problem is, these super-fast, instinctive interpretations are thoughts, not facts, and can be inaccurate, meaning we can feel hurt, upset, or angry unnecessarily. They're called thinking traps because they funnel us down a chain of further unhelpful thoughts, feelings, and actions which can undermine our hope and resilience. This isn't our fault, as it's how the human brain has evolved!

Reflect on the checklist of some common thinking traps below and identify any you tend to fall into or might have caused a recent emotional reaction in you.

I'm not good enough—Tendency to believe you are the cause of every problem; negative self-comparison to others; it's just me.

☐

All or nothing thoughts—Not seeing the shades of gray in between and using words such as "always" and "never."

☐

Mind reading—Assuming you know what someone else is thinking or expecting people to know what you're thinking. ☐

Should/must/ought to—Thoughts that trigger guilt and frustration or disappointment when we think about others. ☐

Believing it's pervasive—Believing that the cause of a problem will spread from one area to negatively affect many other aspects of your life. ☐

Believing it's permanent—Believing negative events are unchangeable; that they'll always stay the same; and that you have little or no control over them. ☐

Blaming "them" or "it"—Blaming other people or circumstances as the cause of every problem. ☐

Are there any other thinking traps you can get caught in? List them below:

_____

_____

_____

How to stop being caught by a thinking trap

When you feel an unpleasant emotional reaction being triggered, pause for a moment and take a breath. Ask yourself: "What's the evidence for my instant interpretation? Are there other possible alternative interpretations? How will I check?" How will you remind yourself to do this? It takes practice, but can help!

My Resilience Role Models

List five people who are role models of resilience, and why you think this is the case. Perhaps they have overcome great difficulty, taken on a huge challenge, or pursued a vision of hope in spite of obstacles. Think of people you know, have read about, or even characters from movies or literature.

Role Model	How is This Person Resilient?
1	
2	
3	
4	
5	

Helpful Hints

Next time you are facing an issue, challenge, or difficulty, pick someone from your list and ask yourself:

- What would this person do in my situation?
- If they were here now, what would their advice be?
- What would be the first step they'd take to tackle this problem?
- Reflecting on this, what's the next step I can take forward in dealing with my issue, challenge, or difficulty?

Find the Best Moment in a Bad Day

In the introduction to this chapter, we explored Dr. Maria Sirois' suggestion that even on the toughest days there will be a moment that is better than the rest. When you're having a really tough time, how might you remind yourself, before you go to sleep each night, to reflect back on the day and find the best (or least bad) moment?

Hope Spotting

"Bad news sells." The media, whether in print or online, is full of stories about pain, suffering, and what's wrong with the world and tends not to highlight solutions or what's actually going well. While it's important to be informed and to feel compassion for others, it's good to have a better balance—to notice positive news and stories of hope, as well as what's wrong, even if we have to work harder to find these.

Over the next few weeks, actively look for 10 stories from close to home or farther afield that inspire hope for you. For example, it might be young people taking action on climate change, a new medical treatment, people who have survived a natural disaster, or coral reefs or burned-down forests regrowing.

List the hopeful stories you've spotted below—with a note of what you find most hopeful in each of them.

Hopeful Story	What Makes It Hopeful to Me?
1	
2	
3	

4 _____   _____

_____   _____

5 _____   _____

_____   _____

6 _____   _____

_____   _____

7 _____   _____

_____   _____

8 _____   _____

_____   _____

9 _____   _____

_____   _____

10 _____   _____

_____   _____

Reflection

- Notice how you feel when reading these stories of hope.

- What's something you are hopeful for right now in your own life?

Soup kitchen
volunteers
needed!

Meaning

Living a happy life is more than simply experiencing pleasurable feelings. It's also about having a sense of meaning and purpose.[69] This has many benefits for our well-being and resilience. For example, studies show it's associated with: experiencing more frequent and stronger positive emotions; having more satisfying relationships; helping others more; higher immunity; better physical and psychological health; increased longevity; and a greater ability to cope with tough times. Feeling life lacks meaning is associated with unhappiness, even distress, but, importantly, research shows there are ways (such as those suggested in this chapter) to help us find it. Meaning can even emerge during, or as a result of, adversity.[70]

So, what does a sense of meaning in life really mean? In simple terms, it's often thought of as feeling connected to, part of, and/or contributing to something bigger or beyond ourselves. Psychologist Dr. Michael Steger, a leading expert on meaning in life, proposes it has three core components:

- **Coherence** (understanding): The sense that the elements of our life fit together and we can make sense of, and have some certainty about, our experience of the world and how we fit into it.

- **Purpose** (motivation): Our sense of direction in life; longer-term aims, aspirations, or intentions we strive toward; and the higher purpose(s) that drive us. This might manifest as goals, but not necessarily. It could be more general, deeply felt intentions, perhaps to be a good parent, friend, and/or romantic partner, or to make a positive contribution in the local community or in our field of work.

- **Significance** (value): Our belief that we and our lives matter and we can make a difference in some small or larger way; that life is worth living or is fulfilling; and living responsibly.[71]

Dr. Paul Dolan, a leading researcher on the science of happiness, argues that we should assess our happiness on the basis of our momentary experiences—not only whether these are pleasurable in some way (or not), but also whether what we're doing or experiencing has purpose or is pointless.[72]

Dr. Steger suggests that finding meaning emerges from reflecting on and interpreting our momentary experiences of the world. This helps to bring the three parts of meaning together—through the process of making connections, interpretations, evaluations, and aspirations—over time and during the course of our lives.[73]

Meaningful Photographs

This is a great way to explore what meaning means for you. Over the next week or so, take 10-12 photographs of things that add a sense of meaning to your life. These could be images of the source of meaning or representative of it. Perhaps places, people, pets, objects, or memorabilia— anything that feels meaningful for you.

Reflect on the images and identify the five most important sources of meaning for you, then list them below. Note how each is meaningful for you. In a study,[74] this activity boosted the participants' sense of meaning and gave them an emotional boost too. How will you nurture these sources of meaning in your life?

My Meaningful Photos	Why the Photo is Meaningful for Me
1	
2	
3	
4	
5	

Many Ways You Make a Difference

Feeling that we contribute to the world can bring a sense of meaning and belonging. Each of us makes a difference to the people and world around us in a myriad of small and bigger ways, even if we don't realize it.

This could be the small ways you care for friends or family, how you make a difference at work, smiling at your neighbors, feeding the birds, growing vegetables, offering constructive support online, contributing to a charity, giving appreciation or compliments, or picking up litter in the park. List all the ways you contribute or make a difference to the world around you, whether in tiny or larger ways.

1

2

3

4

5

6

7

8

9

10

11

12

13

14

15

16

17

18

19

20

Reflection

How does it feel looking back at your list? Over the next few weeks, look for other ways you can make a difference to people and the world around you.

Finding Flow

Flow is the experience of being fully focused on and immersed in an activity. When in flow we are completely absorbed and engaged, time flies, we aren't distracted or self-conscious, and one action flows on from the previous one. Studies show[75] that flow experiences can give us a sense of fulfillment and enjoyment and help us grow and develop.

Activities in which we find flow aren't passive (like watching a video or TV program, even if we're absorbed in it). They are active and involve a level of challenge in what we are doing that just meets or slightly exceeds our current skill level. Typically, it's an activity where we have a clear, immediate goal like playing a song, winning a game, or painting a picture. We vary in the activities in which we find flow. For example, it could be when playing music, sport, or chess, enjoying creative arts, dancing, or climbing.

Think about times when you've experienced flow—what were you doing? When and where were these? List five examples below:

Activity	When and Where Did I Do It?
1	
2	
3	
4	
5	

How did you feel during and after the activities you listed?

Take Action

Pick one of the activities from your list, or another you enjoy doing, then plan when and where you'll do it again. How can you stretch yourself, just enough, and minimize distractions when you do—to enable you to get into flow?

Look Back From the Future

Imagine you are 85 years old and looking back on your life, starting from where you are now into the future. You've felt fulfilled and happy, and your life has given you a sense of meaning. Be hopeful, yet realistic, in your vision of the future and, of course, remember there will probably be challenges along the way. Imagine this life in as much detail as possible.

List below the 10 aspects of your future life vision that were most fulfilling and meaningful for you.

1

2

3

4

5

6

7

8

9

10

Take Action

Pick one aspect from your list. What is the very next step you can take toward creating your future vision? (Make this realistic to ensure it's achievable!) When and where will you be when you do this?

Expand Your Happiness Horizon

What have you learned?

Reflect on what you've explored through using this book. What are three insights you've had about happiness?

1

2

3

Putting it into practice

List three things you've put into practice or done differently in your own life after reading and working through the activities in this book.

1

2

3

Going forward

Looking ahead to the next few months, what is one hopeful, yet realistic, goal you have to help you feel happier and sustain this feeling? Note it down here:

1. Spend a few moments really visualizing what the outcome will be for you when you've taken action to implement your goal. Note down here what you will feel, see, and hear:

2. Identify an obstacle **inside you** that's most likely to get in the way of you achieving this goal:

3. If that obstacle happens, what action can you take to overcome it:

4. Now identify the very next step you'll take toward achieving your goal and when and where you will do this:

Endnotes

Introduction

1 For example: Donaldson, S. I., Cabrera, V., & Gaffaney, J. (2021). Following the Science to Generate Well-Being: Using the Highest-Quality Experimental Evidence to Design Interventions. *Frontiers in psychology*, 12, 739352; Dahl, C. J., Wilson-Mendenhall, C. D., & Davidson, R. J. (2020). The plasticity of well-being: A training-based framework for the cultivation of human flourishing. *Proceedings of the National Academy of Sciences*, 117(51), 32197–32206; Koydemir, S., Sökmez, A. B., & Schütz, A. (2021). A meta-analysis of the effectiveness of randomized controlled positive psychological interventions on subjective and psychological well-being. *Applied Research in Quality of Life*, 16(3), 1145–1185; et al.

2 De Neve, J. E., Diener, E., Tay, L., & Xuereb, C. (2013). The objective benefits of subjective well-being. *World Happiness Report*.

3 For example: Seligman, M. E. (2002). *Authentic Happiness: Using the new positive psychology to realize your potential for lasting fulfilment*, Simon and Schuster; Dolan, P. (2014). *Happiness by Design: Finding Pleasure and Purpose in Everyday Life*, Penguin UK; Ryff, C. D. (2014). Psychological well-being revisited: Advances in the science and practice of eudaimonia. *Psychotherapy and Psychosomatics*, 83(1), 10–28.

4 Fredrickson, B. L. (2013). Positive emotions broaden and build. *Advances In Experimental Social Psychology*, 47, 1–53. Academic Press.

5 Fredrickson, B. L. (2013). Positive emotions broaden and build. *Advances in Experimental Social Psychology*, 47, 1–53. Academic Press.

6 https://www.ons.gov.uk/peoplepopulationandcommunity/wellbeing/methodologies/surveysusingthe4officefornationalstatisticspersonalwellbeingquestions

7 Burton, C. M., & King, L. A. (2008). Effects of (very) brief writing on health: The two-minute miracle. *British Journal of Health Psychology*, 13(1), 9–14; King, L. A. (2001). The health benefits of writing about life goals. *Personality and Social Psychology Bulletin*, 27(7), 798–807.

Gratitude

8 Wood, A. M., Froh, J. J., & Geraghty, A. W. (2010). Gratitude and well-being: A review and theoretical integration. *Clinical Psychology Review*, 30(7), 890–905; Emmons, R. A., & Mishra, A. (2011). Why gratitude enhances well-being: What we know, what we need to know. In K. M. Sheldon, T. B. Kashdan, & M. F. Steger (Eds.), *Designing Positive Psychology: Taking stock and moving forward* (248–262). Oxford University Press; Allen, S. (2018). *The Science of Awe White Paper*. The Greater Good Science Center at UC Berkeley.

9 Emmons, R. A., & McCullough, M. E. (2003). Counting blessings versus burdens: An experimental investigation of gratitude and subjective well-being in daily life. *Journal of Personality and Social Psychology*, 84(2), 377–389.

10 Wood, A. M., Froh, J. J., & Geraghty, A. W. (2010). Gratitude and well-being: A review and theoretical integration. *Clinical Psychology Review*, 30(7), 890–905.

11 Allen, S. (2018). *The Science of Gratitude White Paper*. Greater Good Science Center at U.C. Berkley.

12 Allen, S. (2018). *The Science of Gratitude White Paper*. Greater Good Science Center at U.C. Berkley; Emmons, R. A. (2013). *Gratitude Works!: A 21-day Program for Creating Emotional Prosperity*, John Wiley & Sons.

13 Seligman, M. E., Steen, T. A., Park, N., & Peterson, C. (2005). Positive psychology progress: empirical validation of interventions. *American Psychologist*, 60(5), 410.

14 Seligman, M. E., Steen, T. A., Park, N., & Peterson, C. (2005). Positive psychology progress: empirical validation of interventions. *American Psychologist*, 60(5), 410.

15 Lyubomirsky, S., (2007). *The How of Happiness—A new approach to getting the life you want*, Penguin.

Joy

16 Valliant, G. (2008). *Spiritual Evolution: A Scientific Defense of Faith*, New York, Broadway Books.

17 Johnson, M. K. (2020). Joy: a review of the literature and suggestions for future directions. *The Journal of Positive Psychology*, 15(1), 5–24.

18 Watkins, P. C., Emmons, R. A., Greaves, M. R., & Bell, J. (2018). Joy is a distinct positive emotion: Assessment of joy and relationship to gratitude and well-being. *The Journal of Positive Psychology*, 13(5), 522–539.

19 Johnson, M. K. (2020). Joy: a review of the literature and suggestions for future directions. *The Journal of Positive Psychology*, 15(1), 5–24.

20 Robert A. Emmons (2020). Joy: An introduction to this special issue. *The Journal of Positive Psychology*, 15:1, 1–4.

21 Bryant, F. B., Smart, C. M., & King, S. P. (2005). Using the past to enhance the present: Boosting happiness through positive reminiscence. *Journal of Happiness Studies*, 6(3), 227–260.

22 Based on: Morelli, S. A., Lieberman, M. D., & Zaki, J. (2015). The emerging study of positive empathy. *Social and Personality Psychology Compass*, 9(2), 57–68.

23 Based on: Aknin, L. B., Dunn, E. W., & Norton, M. I. (2012). Happiness runs in a circular motion: Evidence for a positive feedback loop between prosocial spending and happiness. *Journal of Happiness Studies*, 13(2), 347–355; Ko, K., Margolis, S., Revord, J., and Lyubomirsky, S. (2021). Comparing the effects of performing and recalling acts of kindness. *The Journal of Positive Psychology*, 16(1), 73–81.

Peace

24 Ryan, R. M., & Deci, E. L. (2017). *Self-Determination Theory: Basic Psychological Needs in Motivation, Development, and Wellness*, Guilford Publications.

25 Example: van Agteren, J., Lasiello, M., Lo, L., Bartholomaeus, J., Kopsaftis, Z., Carey, M., & Kyrios, M. (2021). A systematic review and meta-analysis of psychological interventions to improve mental wellbeing. *Nature Human Behaviour*, 5(5), 631–652; Dahl, C. J., Wilson-Mendenhall, C. D., & Davidson, R. J. (2020). The plasticity of well-being: A training-based framework for the cultivation of human flourishing. *Proceedings of the National Academy of Sciences*, 117(51), 32197–32206.

26 Hammond, C., & Lewis, G. (2016). The Rest Test: preliminary findings from a large-scale international survey on rest. *The Restless Compendium*, 59–67, Palgrave Macmillan.

27 Huppert, F. (2021). Environment and Well-being. In Grenville-Cleave, B., Guðmundsdóttir, D., Huppert, F., King, V., Roffey, D., Roffey, S., & de Vries, M. (2021). *Creating the World We Want to Live in: How Positive Psychology Can Build a Brighter Future*. Routledge.

28 Example: Yeo, N. L., White, M. P., Alcock, I., Garside, R., Dean, S. G., Smalley, A. J., & Gatersleben, B. (2020). What is the best way of delivering virtual nature for improving mood? An experimental comparison of high definition TV, 360 video, and computer generated virtual reality. *Journal of Environmental Psychology*, 72, 101500.

Curiosity

29 Fredrickson, B. L. (2013). Positive emotions broaden and build. *Advances in Experimental Social Psychology*, 47, 1–53. Academic Press; Fredrickson, B. L. (2009). *Positivity: Groundbreaking research reveals how to embrace the hidden strengths of positive emotions, overcome negativity and thrive*. Crown.

30 Sakaki, M., Yagi, A., & Murayama, K. (2018). Curiosity in old age: a possible key to achieving adaptive aging. *Neuroscience and Biobehavioral Reviews*, 88, 106–116.

31 Sakaki, M., Yagi, A., & Murayama, K. (2018). Curiosity in old age: a possible key to achieving adaptive aging. *Neuroscience and Biobehavioral Reviews*, 88, 106–116.

32 Dweck, C. S. (2008), *Mindset: The New Psychology of Success*, Random House Digital, Inc.

Pride

33 Ryff, C. D. (2014). Psychological well-being revisited: Advances in the science and practice of eudaimonia. *Psychotherapy and Psychosomatics*, 83(1), 10–28.

34 Niemiec, R.M. (2020). Six Functions of Character Strengths for Thriving at Times of Adversity and Opportunity: a Theoretical Perspective. *Applied Research in Quality of Life*, 15, 551–572; Linely, A., Willars, J., & Biswas-Diener, R. (2010). The Strengths Book, CAPP.; Seligman, M. E., Steen, T. A., Park, N., & Peterson, C (2005) Positive psychology progress: empirical validation of interventions. *American Psychologist*, 60(5), 410.

35 Bluth, K. & Neff, K. D. (2018). New frontiers in understanding the benefits of self-compassion. *Self and Identity*, 17(6), 605–608; Neff, K. (2011). *Self Compassion: Stop*

Beating Yourself Up and Leave Insecurity Behind, Hodder & Stoughton.

36 Seligman, M. E., Steen, T. A., Park, N., & Peterson, C. (2005). Positive psychology progress: empirical validation of interventions. *American Psychologist*, 60(5), 410.

37 Neff, K. & Sands, X. (2011), *Self Compassion: Stop Beating Yourself Up and Leave Insecurity Behind*, New York, NY: William Morrow.

Amusement
38 Dunbar, R. I., Baron, R., Frangou, A., Pearce, E., van Leeuwen, E. J., Stow, J., Partridge, G., MacDonald, I., Barra, V., & van Vugt, M. (2012). Social laughter is correlated with an elevated pain threshold. *Proceedings. Biological Sciences*, 279(1731), 1161–1167.

39 Manninen, S., Tuominen, L., Dunbar, R. I., Karjalainen, T., Hirvonen, J., Arponen, E., Hari, R., Jääskeläinen, I. P., Sams, M., & Nummenmaa, L. (2017). Social Laughter Triggers Endogenous Opioid Release in Humans. *The Journal of Neuroscience*, 37(25), 6125–6131.

40 Algoe, S. B. (2019). Positive interpersonal processes. *Current Directions in Psychological Science*, 28(2), 183–188.

41 Algoe, S. B. (2019). Positive interpersonal processes. *Current Directions in Psychological Science*, 28(2), 183–188.

42 Algoe, S. B. (2019). Positive interpersonal processes. *Current Directions in Psychological Science*, 28(2), 183–188.

43 Yuan J. W., McCarthy M., Holley S. R., & Levenson R. W. (2010). Physiological down-regulation and positive emotion in marital interaction. Emotion. 10(4) 467–74; Scott, S. K., Lavan, N., Chen, S., & McGettigan, C. (2014). The social life of laughter. *Trends in Cognitive Sciences*, 18(12), 618–620.

44 Farley, A., Kennedy-Behr, A., & Brown, T. (2021). An Investigation into the Relationship Between Playfulness and Well-being in Australian Adults: An Exploratory Study. *OTJR: Occupation, Participation and Health*, 41(1), 56–64; Proyer, R. T. (2014). Playfulness over the lifespan and its relation to happiness. *Zeitschrift für Gerontologie und Geriatrie*, 47(6), 508–512.

Awe
45 Fredrickson, B. L. (2009). *Positivity: Ground-breaking research reveals how to embrace the hidden strengths of positive emotions, overcome negativity and thrive.* Crown; Allen, S. (2018). *The Science of Awe White Paper* by the Greater Good Science Center at UC Berkeley.

46 Bai, Y., Ocampo, J., Jin, G., Chen, S., Benet-Martinez, V., Monroy, M., Anderson, C., & Keltner, D. (2021). Awe, daily stress, and elevated life satisfaction. *Journal of Personality and Social Psychology*, 120(4), 837–860.

47 Allen, S. (2018). *The Science of Awe White Paper* by the Greater Good Science Center at UC Berkeley.

48 Stellar, J. E., Gordon, A., Anderson, C. L., Piff, P. K., McNeil, G. D., & Keltner, D. (2018). Awe and humility. *Journal of Personality and Social Psychology*, 114(2), 258–269.

49 Allen, S. (2018). *The Science of Awe White Paper* by the Greater Good Science Center at UC Berkeley.

50 Sturm, V. E., Datta, S., Roy, A. R. K., Sible, I. J., et al. (2020). Big smile, small self: Awe walks promote prosocial positive emotions in older adults. Emotion. Advance online publication (https://doi.org/10.1037/emo0000876).

Love
51 Algoe, S. B. (2019). Positive interpersonal processes. *Current Directions in Psychological Science*, 28(2), 183–188.

52 Holt-Lunstad, J., Smith, T. B., Baker, M., Harris, T., & Stephenson, D. (2015). Loneliness and social isolation as risk factors for mortality: a meta-analytic review. *Perspectives on Psychological Science*, 10(2), 227–237.

53 Algoe, S. B. (2019). Positive interpersonal processes. *Current Directions in Psychological Science*, 28(2), 183–188.

54 Fredrickson, B. L. (2016). Love: Positivity resonance as a fresh, evidence-based perspective on an age-old topic. *Handbook of Emotions*, 4, 847–858.

55 Fowler, J. H. & Christakis, N. A. (2008). Dynamic spread of happiness in a large social network: longitudinal analysis over 20 years in the Framingham Heart Study. *BMJ*, 337:a2338

56 Fredrickson, B. L. (2013). *Love 2.0: Finding Happiness and Health in Moments of Connection*, Penguin.

57 Algoe, S. B. (2019). Positive interpersonal processes. *Current Directions in Psychological Science*, 28(2), 183–188; See also King. V. (2016) *10 Keys to Happier Living*. Hachette.

58 Jung, H., Seo, E., Han, E., Henderson, M. D., & Patall, E. A. (2020). Prosocial modeling: A meta-analytic review and synthesis. *Psychological Bulletin*, 146(8), 635; Algoe, S. B., Dwyer, P. C., Younge, A., & Oveis, C. (2020). A new perspective on the social functions of emotions: Gratitude and the witnessing effect. *Journal of Personality and Social Psychology*, 119(1), 40–74.

59 Curry, O. S., Rowland, L. A., Van Lissa, C. J., Zlotowitz, S., McAlaney, J., & Whitehouse, H. (2018). Happy to help? A systematic review and meta-analysis of the effects of performing acts of kindness on the well-being of the actor. *Journal of Experimental Social Psychology*, 76, 320–329.

60 Fredrickson, B. L. (2013). *Love 2.0: Finding Happiness and Health in Moments of Connection*, Penguin.

61 Gable, S. L., Gonzaga, G. C., & Strachman, A. (2006). Will you be there for me when things go right? Supportive responses to positive event disclosures. *Journal of Personality and Social Psychology*, 91(5), 904–917.

62 Lyubomirsky, S., Sheldon, K. M., & Schkade, D. (2005). Pursuing happiness: The architecture of sustainable change. *Review of General Psychology*, 9(2), 111–131.

Hope
63 Fredrickson, B. L. (2013). Positive emotions broaden and build. *Advances in Experimental Social Psychology* (47), 1–53, Academic Press.

64 Waters, L., Algoe, S. B., Dutton, J., Emmons, R., Fredrickson, B. L., Heaphy, E., Moskowitz, J.T., Neff, K., Niemiec, R., Pury, C., & Steger, M. (2021). Positive psychology in a pandemic: buffering, bolstering, and building mental health. *The Journal of Positive Psychology*, 1–21.

65 Waters, L., Algoe, S. B., Dutton, J., Emmons, R., Fredrickson, B. L., Heaphy, E., Moskowitz, J.T., Neff, K., Niemiec, R., Pury, C., & Steger, M. (2021). Positive psychology in a pandemic: buffering, bolstering, and building mental health. *The Journal of Positive Psychology*, 1–21; Ryan, R. M. & Deci, E. L. (2017). *Self-determination theory: Basic psychological needs in motivation, development, and wellness.* Guilford Publications.

66 Quoidbach, J., Wood, A., & Hansenne, M. (2009). Back to the future: The effect of daily practice of mental time travel into the future on happiness and anxiety. *The Journal of Positive Psychology*, (4), 349–355.

67 Aknin, L. B., Van de Vondervoort, J. W., & Hamlin, J. K. (2018). Positive feelings reward and promote prosocial behavior. *Current Opinion in Psychology*, (20), 55–59.

68 Helliwell, J. F., Layard, R., Sachs, J., & De Neve, J. E. (2020). *World Happiness Report.*

Meaning
69 Ryff, C. D. (1989). Happiness is everything, or is it? Explorations on the meaning of psychological well-being. *Journal of Personality and Social Psychology*, (57), 1069–1081; Ryff, C. D., & Singer, B. H. (2008). Know thyself and become what you are: A eudaimonic approach to psychological well-being. *Journal of Happiness Studies*, 9(1), 13–39.; Hone, L. C., Jarden, A., Schofield, G. M., & Duncan, S. (2014). Measuring flourishing: The impact of operational definitions on the prevalence of high levels of wellbeing. *International Journal of Wellbeing* 4(1), 62–90.

70 Waters, L., Algoe, S. B., Dutton, J., Emmons, R., Fredrickson, B. L., Heaphy, E., Moskowitz, J.T., Neff, K., Niemiec, R., Pury, C., & Steger, M. (2021). Positive psychology in a pandemic: buffering, bolstering, and building mental health. *The Journal of Positive Psychology*, 1–21.

71 Martela, F., & Steger, M. F. (2016). The three meanings of meaning in life: Distinguishing coherence, purpose, and significance. *The Journal of Positive Psychology*, 11(5), 531–545.

72 Dolan, P. (2014). *Happiness by Design: Finding Pleasure and Purpose in Everyday Life*, Penguin UK.

73 Martela, F., & Steger, M. F. (2016). The three meanings of meaning in life: Distinguishing coherence, purpose, and significance. *The Journal of Positive Psychology*, 11(5), 531–545.

74 Steger, M. F., Shim, Y., Barenz, J., & Shin, J. Y. (2014). Through the windows of the soul: A pilot study using photography to enhance meaning in life. *Journal of Contextual Behavioral Science*, 3(1), 27–30.

75 Csikzentmihaly, M. (1990), *Flow: The Psychology of Optimal Experience*, New York: Harper & Row.

Further Reading and Resources

If you would like to explore the science of happiness and well-being, and its practical application, further—for yourself and with or for others—below are some suggestions. These are based on Vanessa's work and that of Action for Happiness, the charity and social movement she has been an active part of as Head of Psychology and Workplaces since its launch in 2010.

Other books by Vanessa King

King, V. (2016), *10 Keys to Happier Living: A Practical Handbook for Happiness*, Headline, Hachette (an accessible guide to the science and lots of ideas for action, based on the framework Vanessa developed for Action for Happiness)

Grenville-Cleave, B., Guðmundsdóttir, D., Huppert, F., King, V., Roffey, D., Roffey, S., and de Vries, M. (2021), *Creating the World We Want to Live in: How Positive Psychology Can Build a Brighter Future*, Routledge (inspiration for applying the science of well-being to the different domains of life and society)

For children: King, V., Payne, V., and Harper, P. (2018), *50 Ways to Feel Happy: Fun Activities and Ideas to Build Your Happiness Skills*, Quarto

Get involved: Action for Happiness

Action for Happiness is a not-for-profit social movement based in the UK with a global reach. Its mission is to create a happier, kinder world together. It was founded by leading economist and advocate for measuring societal well-being, Professor, Lord Richard Layard; leading educationalist, Sir Anthony Seldon; and social innovator, Sir Geoff Mulgan.

Action for Happiness share evidence-based resources to help people take action for themselves and together in their communities and facilitate local groups and courses.

Check out the free Action for Happiness resources: monthly calendars to download (tiny daily actions based on the 10 Keys to Happier Living, available in around 40 languages); do the free online 10-day mini course; or sign up to participate in or lead a local group or course.

Join the community at www.actionfor happiness.org.

We can all take action for happiness!

ACTION FOR HAPPINESS

Help if you feel stuck or very unhappy

Many of us will have problems with our mental health at some time in our lives, so if you've been struggling or feeling down for several weeks, suffer from anxiety, depression, or burnout, or are having problems coping, you're not alone. The important thing is not to struggle on without support. Reach out to friends or family members who you trust as soon as you can and let them know you're struggling. Or seek professional advice from your doctor, a qualified psychologist or therapist, or a mental health or counseling helpline. We can sometimes be reluctant to contact our doctor, but please don't be. They will listen and suggest therapies and treatments to help you.

If you are feeling suicidal, it's imperative you reach out to someone you trust *immediately*, such as a friend, family member, colleague, neighbor, or your doctor. In the UK, you can contact the Samaritans 24 hours a day, 365 days of the year (www.samaritans.org) by phoning 116 123 for free. They are there to listen confidentially, whatever you are facing. In the USA, contact local, county, or state support.

Index

Acknowledgments

I'd like to thank Jo Lightfoot for commissioning me to write this book; Claudia Young and Imogen Morrell at Greene and Heaton for making it happen; Caroline West, editor and amazing project manager; and the supportive and positive team at Dorling Kindersley, especially Izzy Merry, Jo Connor, and Peter Jorgensen. And, of course, Tasha Goddard, whose hard work on the illustrations has brought the book to life.

This book, and my broader work with communities and workplaces, would not be possible without the dedicated research of countless academics in the field of positive psychology and beyond who are dedicated to exploring what enables us to live happy, flourishing lives.

I'd also like to acknowledge my colleagues and the volunteers at Action for Happiness: Mark Williamson, Sarah Vero, Alex Nunn, Rachel Fitzgerald, Tanya Barrett, Peter Harper, Val Payne, Tracy Ampah, Gaby Deschamps, Joshua French, Nikki Shaw, David Smart, and Suzy Dion, among others, whose hard work is helping to catalyze the application of the science of happiness to make a positive difference in a growing number of communities around the world.

Special thanks also to Jane Gaukroger for her wise counsel and to Damion Wonfor for holding space for me to think when I need it. The past 18 months have shown me, more than ever, that I am blessed with truly good friends, including Jane (above), Jacqueline Otten, Karen and Neil Gallacher, and Kelly Stuck. Thank you for all your help during a challenging year of change. I've truly appreciated it.

Importantly, I'd like to express my profound gratitude and appreciation to my partner John, who has been there supporting me, even when that's not easy.